D0444967

Where I Come From

Essential Poets Series 64

Maria Mazziotti Gillan

Where I Come From

Selected and New Poems

Guernica
Toronto / New York
1995

© Maria Mazziotti Gillan and Guernica Editions Inc. 1995.
All rights reserved.

Antonio D'Alfonso, Editor.
Guernica Editions Inc.
P.O. Box 117, Station P, Toronto (Ontario), Canada M5S 2S6.
340 Nagel Drive, Cheektowaga, N.Y., 14225-4731 U.S.A.

Typesetting by Jean Yves Collette.
Printed in Canada.

Legal Deposit – Second Quarter
National Library of Canada.

Library of Congress Catalog Card Number: 93-73687

Canadian Cataloguing in Publication Data

Gillan, Maria M.
Where I come from : selected and new poems

(Essential poets ; 64)
ISBN 1-55071-005-2

I . Title.   II . Series.

PS3557 . I375W44 1994   811' . 54   C94 - 900104 - X

Contents

Betrayals

At thirteen, I screamed,
"You're disgusting,"
drinking your coffee from a saucer.
Your startled eyes darkened with shame.

You, one dead leg dragging,
counting your night-shift hours,
You, smiling past yellowed, gaping teeth,
You, mixing the eggnog for me yourself
in a fat dime store cup,

How I betrayed you,
over and over, ashamed of your broken tongue,
how I laughed, savage and innocent,
at your mutilations.

Today, my son shouts,
"Don't tell anyone you're my mother,"
hunching down in the car
so the other boys won't see us together.

Daddy, are you laughing?
Oh, how things turn full circle.
My own words coming back
to slap my face.

I was sixteen when you called one night from your work.
I called you "dear,"

loving you in that moment
past all the barriers of the heart.
You called again every night for a week.
I never said it again.
I wish I could say it now.

Dear, my Dear,
with your twisted tongue,
I did not understand you
dragging your burden of love.

1980

Letter to My Son

The weeks tumble over themselves
since you've been gone. The leaves
fall from the oaks.
The air turns damp and biting,
the sky gray as an old blanket.

We are unchanged, moving
in our accustomed circles.
You miles away, have grown into a man
I can be proud of; but when you call,
I feel I am speaking to a person
hidden behind a screen. I remember

you as a little boy, your legs chunky,
your eyes gray and dreamy as a Turner
landscape. A figure moves toward you,
a younger version of myself.
She holds your hand. You speak.

Other scenes appear. She stands
at the bottom of the stairs,
calls "In a minute, in a minute,"
till your eyes close in sleep.

The weeks go by.
You spin your life into shape.
Now it is you who chant,
"In a minute, in a minute,"
and I who taste salt on my tongue.

The Paper Dolls

To my sister Laura

Darked-eyed Julio laughed his way
into our house, swung me in air.
He said: "This one is my girl"
and "I'll wait for you. Will you marry me?"

I held my mother's hand
when he married.
I never looked at his bride
or said their names.
On the way out of the church,
past confetti and congratulations,
I threw up on Mrs. Gianelli's fur coat.
She never forgave me.

We ate fresh snow with espresso on it,
sugar sprinkled on top. Nothing since
has tasted so good.

Your breasts grew first.
You were older, destined for 36D.
I wondered why you weren't ashamed.
My own grew round as oranges, then stopped.
I was glad.

No matter what you did, men grabbed
at you, cornered you in hallways
and kitchens, thought your breasts
were a sign, wanted to drink,

to unsnap your bra.
I followed you everywhere.
We rode in Carmela's old Ford
through Bergen County dreaming.
Dreaming the lovely houses were ours,
dreaming a prince would save us.

Now in your September kitchen, I watch you
twist your hands. We are close
though we rarely speak. Those rides
in summer and winter, hopes that beat
like caged birds in our hearts,
remain stored in boxes, the lids
never open. Your body is twisted by disease;
mine bends forward as though I wait for blows.

Once I envied your breasts
as you envied my poems.
Life has flattened us both out,
turned us into cardboard figures
like our paper dolls
stiff and easily torn.

Public School No. 18
Paterson, New Jersey

Miss Wilson's eyes, opaque
as blue glass, fix on me:
"We must speak English.
We're in America now."
I want to say, "I am American,"
but the evidence is stacked against me.

My mother scrubs my scalp raw, wraps
my shining hair in white rags
to make it curl. Miss Wilson
drags me to the window, checks my hair
for lice. My face wants to hide.

At home, my words smooth in my mouth,
I chatter and am proud. In school,
I am silent, grope for the right English
words, fear the Italian word
will sprout from my mouth like a rose,

fear the progression of teachers
in their sprigged dresses,
their Anglo-Saxon faces.

Without words, they tell me
to be ashamed.
I am.
I deny that booted country
even from myself,

want to be still
and untouchable
as these women
who teach me to hate myself.

Years later, in a white
Kansas City house,
the Pyschology professor tells me
I remind him of the Mafia leader
on the cover of *Time* magazine.

My anger spits
venomous from my mouth:

I am proud of my mother,
dressed all in black,
proud of my father
with his broken tongue,
proud of the laughter
and noise of our house.

Remember me, Ladies,
the silent one?
I have found my voice
and my rage will blow
your house down.

1984

My Daughter at Fourteen:
Christmas Dance, 1981

Panic in your face, you write questions
to ask him. When he arrives,
you are serene, your fear
unbetrayed. How unlike me you are.

After the dance,
I see your happiness; he holds
your hand. Though you barely speak,
your body pulses messages I can read

all too well. He kisses you goodnight,
his body moving toward yours, and yours
responding. I am frightened, guard my
tongue for fear my mother will pop out

of my mouth. "He is not shy," I say. You giggle,
a little girl again, but you tell me he
kissed you on the dance floor. "Once?"
I ask. "No, a lot."

We ride through rain-shining 1 a.m.
streets. I bite back words which long
to be said, knowing I must not shatter your
moment, fragile as a spun-glass bird,

you, the moment, poised on the edge of
flight, and I, on the ground, afraid.

Awakening

I wake slowly, closed against the eyes
of morning. Your pillow is still warm.
The children sleep, flushed and damp,
in their beds.

The clock ticks smoothly.
The milk glasses wait in the sink.

My mother got up early
in the frozen mornings.

My day's dawning was her
eyes and hands loving me awake.

In memory, the farina still steams.
The stove murmurs. The bread
rises sweetly in its bowl.
I am safe in a circle of love.

The oak creaks and is silent.
My rooms are still.

Listen for my heartbeat.
Am I breathing?

1980-84

The Shadow Rushing to Meet Us

For Jennifer

My just turned fourteen was novels
through which I dreamed my hours away, and
an innocence ferocious in its blindness.
My fourteen was Sinatra records and Billy
Eckstein's syrupy voice and long gray skirts
that stopped just short of rolled bobby socks.
My fourteen was shiny little girl hair,
no style springing curly hair.

Your fourteen is Vanderbilt jeans and
Sassoon shirts, your blonde hair
perfectly ironed into curls, your cornflower
eyes, the lids blue-shadowed, bright
as sun-beaten glass. Your woman
body sends animal signals I have not learned, even now.

Yet when I drive through the dark Allendale streets
to pick you up from the dance, in the carlight,
your face, eyes are taut, shuttered. We drop Colleen
at her house. You cry. The opaque veil in
your eyes melts.

I remember a dance, a high school dance...
I stood all night on the sidelines alone. The smile
scaled from my face like old glue. My new red blouse
and plaid skirt could not cover my nakedness
as I, standing stupidly, no longer even trying

to smile, brushed away tears
as you do now. Watching your face, pleated
with anguish, I see that my fourteen and yours
are not so far apart after all. We sit in our
kitchen. I hold you, smooth away your tears,

try to tell you how we all come to it
in the end, the brick wall, the shadow
rushing to meet us.

So it is not so bad to cry now here in my arms, safe...
a dress rehearsal for the real tears
which will come sure as rain.

Jennifer

Under the luscent skin,
the fine bones, your mind,
fierce and sharp, bites
into questions while
your quick heart cries
for all lame things,
yet you fear your beauty
is only an accident
of genes colliding.

"But when they know me,"
you say, "when they know me,
they won't like me."

Daughter, hear me.
I proclaim your loveliness,
clutching your poems
in your hand, breathing
fire, I draw closer, warm
my cold hands, want
to remember you like this,
so alive I could strike
a match off your face.

Letter to My Mother: Past Due

Today you tell me your mother appears
to you in dreams, but she is always
angry. "You're wrong," she screams.
You see her as a sign;
when she visits your nights, a cloud
of catastrophe bursts on your house.

Ma, hearing you tell me about her,
I see you, for a moment, as a young
girl, caught in a mahogany frame,
a young girl in a thirties wedding
dress with a crown of flowers in your
hair, your eyes deep and terrified,

see you leaning on the rail of that phantom
ship, waving one last goodbye, think
of you, writing to her, year after year,
sending her stilted photographs of your
children, a photo of yourself, your body
young and firm in a flowered dress.

You never saw her again.
She comes to you now only in dreams, angry she
comes. Did she, once, show her love as you
do, scolding, always scolding, yet always
there for me as no one else has ever been?

Once, twenty years ago, a young man bought
my dinner (oysters and wine and waiters
with white cloths draped over their arms),
forced his way into my room in that seedy
Baltimore hotel, insisted he would teach me
how to love, and as I struggled, you called,
asked, "What's wrong? I know something's
wrong." I didn't understand how you could
have known.

Yet even now, you train your heart on us like radar,
sensing our pain before we know it ourselves
as I train my heart on my children.

Promise me, Ma, promise to come to me in dreams,
even scolding, to come to me though I have been angry
with you too often, though I have asked you
to leave me alone. Come to me in dreams,
knowing I loved you
always, even when I hurled my rage in your face.

To Zio Guillermo: in Memorium

I forget him for years,
his shadow kindling on sunset,
his voice gravelly, his hands,
nicotine-stained and calloused,
shaping a silver ball for me

out of cigarette papers, first
small, then layer on layer, our
days silvered, the Camels consumed,
one after the other, his hands
never free of the curling smoke,

his warm smoke smell. In the summer
evenings, his hands carve intricate
bird houses, scrolled and latticed,
and wind pointers, black birds with
whirling wings. Curls of pine

beard his feet. His eyes say
I am all he has of child, this godfather
uncle, his harridan wife shoving him
through days, his eyes mild and sad.

Though he is dead now ten years,
I see him still, rustling through
corn in our bright patchwork garden,
bending over zinnias and marigolds,
calling the birds home.

1981

Image in a Curved Glass

Janet of the freckles and the pale white skin,
Janet of the board body and knobby knees,
I remember your eyes, round and dark as raisins,
your father, runty and plain, just like you.

In your little room, we whispered behind closed doors,
laughed into mirrors, clutched our hoped-for beauty
and ventured out into the sun. We never talked
about your grandmother dying in the room next to yours,
her eyes blazing, the stench permeating the hall,

or your step-mother who blossomed
miraculously with child. What did you think
of as you lay in that iron bed in your lopsided little
house with its thin walls? You never said.

In your lace graduation dress stretched
tight across bud breasts, your face was plain as
          a plank wearing lank brown hair.
That summer you moved to Pompton Lakes,
I took the bus to visit you once
and you showed me your new house, small and
          narrow as the
Thirteenth Street one, but with a brook out back
          where we ate watermelon

dripping seeds into sweet grass. We walked the town's
crooked streets while you whispered that you had a
       boyfriend named Ron
and you loved him. Two years later, when my life
       had filled out
with friends and school, you came to visit. We went
       together to the
Blue Stamp Redemption Center where you turned in
       your hoarded books
for an iron and talked of plans to marry Ron and of
       waiting for his
letters though sometimes they did not come. Your
       life seemed to me
then strange as a Martian's yet even in my
       separateness, I saw your loneliness
like a rift in the sky, saw a vision of your Pompton house

where your stepmother gave birth interminably to
       babies who
squeezed you out until you drifted away. Even then,
       I knew you had
done it already but I did not ask. We never talked
       about the things
that mattered. The cells of thirty years have been
       brushed from my hands

yet I wonder still: Did he marry you? Did you pop
       one child
after another in rented rooms?

Eulogy to Blasberg's Farm

We used to reach it, take our
bikes up Lynack Road, pause
at gravestones in the bramble-
bushed cemetery, stones old and
fallen, wild flowers growing over
them in tangled clumps.

We sat cross-legged on the grass,
drinking our Cokes, preparing
for a journey whose distances
we could not even begin to measure.

Up Lynack Road into the back gate
of Blasberg's, we rode the crooked
rows, drowning in scented
apples, deep and scarlet
against a lilac-colored sky.

We careened down
the road, spring flying behind
us like a cloak, unaware that one
day we would mourn the tangled
underbrush, the lost curve
of apple trees, the blue
untarnished sky.

1983

Waiting for the Results of a Pregnancy Test

At forty-one, I am uncertain of more things
than I could have imagined twenty years ago.

Your existence or non-existence
hovers over me today. The voices
of the world my friends the liberated
women who are close to me cry
abort abort abort in unison.

Yet the voice inside me shouts
          No

shows my selfishness in its mirror
my soul's dark intent.

This newt, this merging of tiny cells
makes an explosion like comets
colliding in my ordered universe.

I want to say: I'm too old, too tired,
too caught up in trying wings so long unused,
but that voice will not be silent. It beats
in my bones with its primitive insistence.

Little life, floating in your boat of cells,
I will carry you under my heart
though the arithmetic is against us both.

Today I bypass the baby departments,
the thousand reminders that come to me now.
The young women wheeling strollers through

Bradlees, the girl in the maternity shirt
which proclaims: "I'm not lonely anymore."

I want to scream, we are all born lonely,
and the child beating under our hearts
does not change that. I want to lie down
on the ugly pebbled floor of Bradlees and kick
my feet and pound my fists and make this intruder
in my life vanish.

As I stand at the checkout line, I see our years unroll:

the bottles
midnight feedings
tinker toys
baseball games
PTA meetings

are boulders in my path, a mountain
of boulders I will have to climb
for you. I walk into the spring sunlight
while my life snaps closed around me and my fear.

My friends are all my age, their children in high
school
as mine are. I will be alone with you.
You will be born with a scowl on your face,
your hands shaking, having taken from the marrow
of my bones my own quaking.

We will rock together in this leaky boat and
I will love you, I know; it is only in these first
moments, while I alter the picture of my life
I had painted with such sure strokes, only in these
moments that I wish you were not there.

In New Jersey Once

In New Jersey once, marigolds grew wild.
Fields swayed with daisies.
Oaks stood tall on mountains.
Powdered butterflies graced the velvet air.

Listen. It was like that.
Before the bulldozers.
Before the cranes.
Before the cement sealed the earth.

Even the stars, which used to hang
in thick clusters in the black sky,
even the stars are dim.

Burrow under the blacktop,
under the cement, the old dark earth
is still there. Dig your hands into it,
feel it, deep, alive on your fingers.

Know that the earth breathes and pulses still.
Listen. It mourns. In New Jersey once, flowers grew.

Poem to John:
Freshman Year, Drew University, 1983

You've been gone now four weeks.
It seems like forever.
You say you'll call.
I wait near the phone
so I won't miss you.
The phone stays mute.

I feel the way I did
when I let you walk home
from kindergarten
and you were late.

Only now you're grown-up
and you're doing fine.
I'm the one who can't let go,
who can't stop trying to help you,
who can't stop

trying
because you're grown-up
and I have to not
remind you to get your shot,
and I have to not bring you blankets
and peanut butter and potato chips
and chocolate chip cookies

and I have to keep my voice down
when I see you making the same mistakes
I made.
I sit near the phone, waiting,
needing to hear from you
but not wanting to shame you by calling.
The truth is you're more grown-up
than I am, and I'll try to believe
what I know already. You'll be fine
without me. You'll be fine.

Dawn

Here, in the early morning,
with rain running from the
gutters, the loneliness

fits like a comfortable coat
and the quiet, familiar creakings
of the house are part of me.

I am soothed by them, the sounds and
stirrings, water in the bath,
my son's footsteps on the stairs.

The sleeves of this coat are warm
on my skin. My house of bones rests
calm and singing a music all its own.

The Onion

To Robert Bly

Shaded in layers from burnt umber to pumpkin to
gold, this onion curves upward in a graceful arc, the
line of a womb perhaps or the shape people draw to
represent women. Curved and rounded in on itself,
only one burnt orange strip of skin, frail as parch-
ment, flaps loose, pointing down and away. The rest,
layer on layer, protects its heart. I am like that,
private as a bud, wound tight, circling in on itself.

We are all like that, yet peel us away, one layer at a
time, and underneath, at the core, each of us with a
secret to tell, burning under the bleached scalp. I
hold this earth fruit in my hand. Pumpkin-colored
lines flow upward toward the tip, never wavering in

their journey as though flowing from some hidden
river. Why are we so much more than we appear to
be? Touch the veined skin, the cool roundness. We
cannot know its secrets. It does not murmur as a
shell murmurs; it keeps to itself, wrapped in its thin
skin, frail and ferocious as a sparrow. Even the stars
dim watching us, our backs to the wall.

1981

Stereopticon

All the people from my past come to sit with me tonight in my bright suburban kitchen, Ma, in her rocker, holding me still, telling her stories, and Daddy like dark wine, and Laura, her laugh clear as a crystal bell, and Al, his small brown hand in mine, and Zia Louisa with her huge chocolate squares, and Zia Rosa, the nights under the grape arbor, its summer sweet smell, and Zia Amalia, the mole on her nose, her foot tapping its nervous rhythm, and Zia Christina, her chickens in the garbage while we ate farina, and all the others who crowd in on me tonight while I think of my pink bedroom, cheap pink of cheap paint, and the pipes in the bathroom and the wallpaper Ma bought, how lovely it was, and even with it up, the bathroom ugly, and the linoleum in the dining room and the sofabed for Al and crowded and Molly whose husband stopped sleeping with her when she got cancer you know where and he said she wasn't a woman anymore and she cried and cried. How they crowd in on me tonight. How rich I was, though I didn't know it then.

1981

Morning in New Jersey

Morning in New Jersey. Houses
and leaning oaks.

I pull this gray day toward me,
hear the insistent pulse of earth
knocking in its arched room.

I reach to touch it. My hand finds
only brown branch and misty air.

Under my fingers, I feel a movement
so slight I am not certain it is there
and a warm center as if a volcano

were burning deep underground.

1982

Oak Place Musings

I

On my neighbor's roof, plastic butterflies
freeze in rigid postures. Rubber ducks waddle
into trimmed evergreens; plaster cats climb
siding toward peaked roofs.

Once, in a vacant Paterson lot, I caught
a butterfly; the lot seemed huge. Daisies
grew there and marigolds and red berries
which stained our fingers. We had crepe paper
whirlers in varied colors; we spun and spun.
The whirlers were an army of insects
buzzing, till tall grass and flowers blurred.

The butterfly in my hand beat its wings
in terror. My hand stained gold.
When I let it escape it flew away fast,
and then, forgetting, it dipped and swirled
so gracefully I almost stopped breathing.

II

By 9 each morning, Oak Place with its neat box
houses lies still and empty. Children have vanished
into yellow camp buses, parents departed in separate cars.

The street settles into somnolence. Its lines
and angles imprison handkerchief lawns
until even the old oaks no longer seem at home.
In my yesterdays I dreamed myself out of the old city,
imagining a world just like this one,
away from strewn garbage and houses stacked close
        as teeth.

Today I mourn tomatoes ripening in our immigrant
        gardens,
the pattern of sun on walls of old brick mills,
a time when each day opened like a morning glory.
Some days when I look at my hand, I imagine
it is still stained gold.

1985

After the Children Leave Home

Slowly, we settle into the quiet house.
We almost grow accustomed to the noise
of absence, that terrible stillness
that slides along carpeted surfaces.
"The house is so quiet without them,"
you say, your voice husky with loss.

For years, we have adjusted ourselves
to their schedules, the nights of fever
and coughing, the days of car pools
and tinker toys, PTA meetings
and homework, our time together
torn by their needs.

Now facing each other across this empty
landscape, we are vulnerable
as creatures suddenly bereft of skin.
Somewhere along the way, caught in our busyness,
we lost the habit of speech,
the pathways leading to the secrets
of the heart. So we begin
slowly our grave dance, moving
through the braille of touch
into that textured country
where words are unnecessary.
Our bodies give warmth and comfort
as we struggle to reinvent the language
through which we name ourselves.

Love Poem to My Husband

From the lobby
of the Best Western Motel
in Ontario, California,
I watch the cars speed by
on the two-lane highway,
and think of you.

Yesterday, I flew across
3,000 miles of sky,
the country below
blurred by clouds,
and then to Ontario airport,
long and open like no airport
I've ever seen,
and to this motel
in the middle of honking horns
and roar of plane
motors. The farther
I move away from you,
the more you are with me.
I am cut adrift,
here alone for a week
I don't know how I'll live through.
The heat oppresses me
and the thought of you
so far away.

Here, these cars, this noise,
this sun that shimmers
on asphalt teach me more
than years in our yellow house.
I was too close to see;
only now do I learn,
without you a part of me
that flies and sings dies.

I can feel the soft, clean smell
of your skin, your hands
as you kissed me goodbye,
your eyes, dark with worry,
not wanting to let me go.

Love,
forgive my inattention,
my yearning for a freedom
I do not want.

The Morse Code of Love

On the New Jersey Turnpike, I drive
toward the Barron Art Center.
The refineries spew acrid smoke
over the houses and people.
I wonder, do those who live here
stop smelling the odor that makes me
want to hold my breath
till I've passed Elizabeth?

I get off the Turnpike,
follow signs to Route 9,
lose the exit
and drift through grimy, honky-tonk
towns lined with McDonald's and Burger King,
Goodrich Tires and Hess Gas Stations.

When I arrive at the reading, the Center
is not air-conditioned, and we are crowded
into a small room. My friend, the poet,
reads well, savoring the drama of his words.
Sometimes another friend accompanies him
on the flute, the sound plaintive and sad
in the still air. I think of Jennifer
alone in Washington and wish I had not missed
her call. I try to imagine her
sleeping in her dorm room trying
to make it lovely. I wonder if her

boyfriend has delivered the final axe stroke.
As I drive through Niagaras of rain past Rahway State
       Prison
and bars that are seedy and neon-lit, I look for signs
that seem to have vanished, and call out to her
in the Morse Code of love. Daughter, imagine
that I am holding you and that this loneliness, too,
can be soothed and comforted.

Uncertainties

When seen from the window
of TWA's Flight Number 171,
the clouds are thick as banks of snow.
I swear I could step out of this window
and walk thigh-deep in snow
just as the children did
in the winters
of long ago.

I remember when the ground seemed so firm
beneath my feet, when I was sure
I knew exactly where I'd be
a year from then. Today the path ahead
is like those clouds; it appears to be solid;
yet, if I were to lift the heavy door that guards us
and step outside this window,
I would meet the cavern
of empty space
into which I'd fall.

Talismans

I

Each day, Miss Elmer wore
a different flowered silk dress,
a cameo at the neck, a small
white collar. She smelled dusty
as though she had been left
too long in a closet.
Crack! went her ruler across our hands.
Crack! Crack! against small white knuckles.
"Hold out your hands," and our hands trembled.

II

Thinking of myself in second grade
and of Miss Elmer, I see,
from a world far removed from tenements
and naked bathroom pipes,
my mother's face, serious and intent,
as she pins an evil-eye horn
and scapula to my undershirt. Wearing them,
I am sure I can go out into the world
protected.

Now, when walking out of the house
each morning has become an act of courage,
I wish I could feel them there still,
breathing next to my skin.

This Shell

For Robert Bly

This shell, this delicate fan, is fluted with alternating brown and white lines curved out from the center and at the top, frail white wings, transparent as fine china. On its underside, a circle of mottled earth color, autumn leaf color, arcs over a white bowl with a tan center. I imagine the bowl holds milk and that some child might pretend it is a cup for a doll, might make a tea party with them, a circle of small shell cups, and suddenly I remember a birthday party. It is my twelfth birthday, and my friends sit around our table, laughing and pretending to be grown-up. There are no boys at this party, so the girls do not really want to be here. But, not to hurt my feelings, they have come. My mother, small and compact, bustles around us, serving our food. Without warning, my mother slaps me so hard the mark of her fingers remains on my face. I do not know what I said to provoke her anger. I only remember the party before, perfect and formed like the fluted shell; and the party after, broken, and myself, growing more transparent with each moment.

Christmas Shopping For My Mother
December, 1985

You, with your craving for order,
   with your delicate touch,
   with your small-boned hands
that keep us from harm.

I want to give you something
so beautiful it will be exactly
what you have always wanted,
something to make up for
the five and dime ornaments
you made do with
all those Paterson years.

In memory, I see you
in the old, brown rocker,
your needle moving rhythmically
in and out of sleeves
of huge army coats,
see you, long after we are in bed,
pulling basting stitches,
till a pile of thread covers your feet,

see your hands scrubbing clothes
on the tin washboard, your face intent
and lined even at thirty,
remember you ironing our clothes
to crispness under the light
of a dim bulb.

I want to give you
a diamond to make up for
the one you never had,
days sunny with leisure.

I leave Meyer Brothers's aisle,
step out into frigid December air,
knowing there is nothing I can buy for you.

I bow to your courage
and your back that was never broken
or bent, no matter what,
and bring you, instead, this poem.

1985-86

Maria
Mazziotti
Gillan

God Is Not Easy

God is not easy
like the plastic Jesus
you put on the dashboard
who glows in the dark
so you can always find him.

If he were easy,
I could slip him
in and out of a little velvet
purse whenever I wanted
him and put him back
when I didn't.

I wish he were easy
like my mother's God
who comes to her
whenever she asks
and sends her bluejays
that sing in January
so she'll know he's there.

God is
complex as the ear of the cat,
hard as the pit
in an unripened peach.

If only God would stay
in the Tabernacle, I could open

the little gold door any time
of the day or night
and there he'd be,
small and smiling,
safe as a chicken
or a goose.

Sometimes when my heart
is a dumb stone and webs
of grief catch in my eyelids,
he hands me a mountain,
alight with autumn,
or the sudden white petals
on a Japanese Cherry tree.

But God is smoke or air;
whenever I think I've caught him,
he escapes through my fingers.
I am left holding
emptiness,
a blank space
that can never be filled.

1987

Mrs. Sinnegan's Dogwood

I

On this morning in May,
Mrs. Sinnegan's dogwood
suddenly blossoms all white lace,
a delicate tracery
that filters light.

Each spring, I watch this tree
for the moment of silver light
when the long sleep ends and the words
that have lain dormant in darkness
rise from ashes.

II

I remember the Japanese cherry tree that bowed
just outside my window; for years
the scent of blossoms perfumed my dreams.
I see the trees, the one inextricably woven
into the years of my growing; the other
tied to middle age, a double image,
iridescent and floating.

Mrs. Sinnegan drags her chair down her back steps,
one trembling hand on her walker,
the other pulling a metal lawn chair.
She positions her chair
so she can see the tree.

At eighty her bright eyes fade to pale blue,
and her words crawl.
Yet her heart
leaps through meadows
of clover and Queen Anne's lace.

III

This year, the dogwood blooms for weeks
like a special gift.
The leaves make patterns
on the roof. The birds gather
at the feeder and then perch on the edge
of my window, singing.
One day, Mrs. Sinnegan says the tree
looks like a girl in a communion veil;
another, like a bride pulling her satin train.
Today I imagine the tree is a matron
in a flowered hat.

Arturo

I told everyone
your name was Arthur,
tried to turn you
into the imaginary father
in the three-piece suit
that I wanted instead of my own.
I changed my name to Marie,
hoping no one would notice
my face with its dark Italian eyes.

Arturo, I send you this message
from my younger self, that fool
who needed to deny
the words
(Wop! Guinea! Greaseball!)
slung like curved spears,
the anguish of sandwiches
made from spinach and oil;
the roasted peppers on homemade bread,
the rice pies of Easter.

Today, I watch you,
clean as a cherub,
your ruddy face shining,
closed by your growing deafness
in a world where my words
cannot touch you.

At eighty, you still worship
Roosevelt and J.F.K.,
read the newspaper carefully,
know with a quick shrewdness
the details of revolutions and dictators,
the cause and effect of all wars,
no matter how small.
Only your legs betray you
as you limp from pillar to pillar,
yet your convictions remain
as strong now as they were at twenty.
For the children, you carry chocolates
wrapped in gold foil
and find for them always
your crooked grin and a five-dollar bill.

I smile when I think of you.
Listen, America,
this is my father, Arturo,
and I am his daughter, Maria.
Do not call me Marie.

The Young Men In Black Leather Jackets

Today I am reminded
of the young men
who stood for hours
in front of the candy store
on 19th Street and 2nd Avenue
in Paterson, New Jersey,
the young men in black leather
jackets and tough faces,
their ducktail haircuts identical,
the young men who stared with hard
bright eyes at the girls passing by
and made comments like "Here chickie, chickie,
c'mere, chickie," their laughter following us
down the street.

One day, as I dreamed my way through
one of the long novels I loved,
their footsteps sounded on the pavement.
The three of them walked in perfect step,
their long legs scissoring as they sang
in their loudest voices:

> *My Bonnie lies over the ocean.*
> *My Bonnie lies over the sea.*
> *My mother lies over my father's knee*
> *And that's how they got little me.*

For years, I remember their song,
the look of terrible mockery in their eyes,
their hatred of women and their need of them.
I remember that it was August. Late. Almost time
for school again. They are seventeen or eighteen;
I am thirteen.
I do not understand their song; I only know
I am ashamed as though I, and not they,
had done wrong.

Growing up Italian

When I was a little girl,
I thought everyone was Italian,
and that was good. We visited
our aunts and uncles,
and they visited us.
The Italian language smooth
and sweet in my mouth.

In kindergarten, English words fell on me,
thick and sharp as hail. I grew silent,
the Italian word balanced on the edge
of my tongue and the English word, lost
during the first moment
of every question.

It did not take me long to learn
that dark-skinned people were greasy
and dirty. Poor children were even dirtier.
To be dark-skinned and poor was to be dirtiest of all.

Almost every day
Mr. Landgraf called Joey
a "spaghetti bender."
I knew that was bad.
I tried to hide
by folding my hands neatly
on my desk and
being a good girl.

Judy, one of the girls in my class,
had honey-blonde hair and blue eyes.
All the boys liked her. Her parents and
grandparents were born in America.
They owned a local tavern.
When Judy's mother went downtown,
she brought back coloring books and candy.
When my mother went downtown, she brought back
one small brown bag with a towel or a sheet in it.

The first day I wore my sister's hand-me-down coat,
Isabelle said, "That coat looks familiar. Don't
I recognize that coat?" I looked at the ground.

When the other children brought presents
for the teacher at Christmas, embroidered silk
handkerchiefs and "Evening in Paris" perfume,
I brought dishcloths made into a doll.

I read all the magazines that told me
why blondes have more fun,
described girls whose favorite color was blue.
I hoped for a miracle that would turn my dark skin light,
that would make me pale and blonde and beautiful.

So I looked for a man
with blond hair and blue eyes
who would blend right in,
and who'd give me blond, blue-eyed children
who would blend right in
and a name that would blend right in
and I would be melted down

to a shape and a color
that would blend right in,
till one day, I guess I was forty by then,

I woke up cursing
all those who taught me
to hate my dark, foreign self,

and I said, "Here I am –
with my olive-toned skin
and my Italian parents,
and my old poverty,
real as a scar on my forehead,"
and all the toys we couldn't buy
and all the words I didn't say,
all the downcast eyes
and folded hands
and remarks I didn't make
rise up in me and explode

onto paper like firecrackers
                    like meteors
and I celebrate
                    my Italian American self,
rooted in this, my country, where
all those black/brown/red/yellow
olive-skinned people
soon will raise their voices
and sing this new anthem:

Here I am
        and I'm strong

and my skin is warm in the sun
and my dark hair shines,

and today, I take back my name
and wave it in their faces
like a bright, red flag.

In Memory We Are Walking

In memory we are walking
single file, up Goffle Road.

We are carrying an old red blanket
and tin buckets
that clang against each other
as we move.

We have been walking for more than an hour.
At last, we stop, sit for a moment
on grass and drink the lemonade
my mother made before we left home.

Then with my mother shouting commands
like a general, we spread out the blanket
under a mulberry tree, each of us taking
a corner, my father shaking the limbs
of the tree. Huge purple fruit
fall thick and noisy as hail.

We laugh and capture mulberries
until the blanket sags with the weight.
Delicately, my mother scoops mulberries
into our buckets, gives us each
some to eat.

We walk along the brook,
watch the water rush
over rocks, and follow

the brook toward home.
I am ten years old.
I have seldom been out of Paterson.

The houses we pass,
squat, middle-class bungalows,
seem to be the houses
of the wealthy when seen through
my eyes.

On the way back, my brother is tired;
he drags behind, until my father
puts him on his shoulders. My legs hurt,
but I would not say it for the world.
I am happy. I do not know
that in the houses neighboring the park
people have watched us. They hate
our dark skin, our immigrant clothes.

My father tells us that, a few years before,
he walked all the way to Passaic and back,
following the railroad tracks
because he heard there was a job open.
He did not have five cents for the train.

When he got to Passaic, the foreman
told him there were no jobs. The workers
turned to watch him leave,
their eyes strong as hands on his back.
"You stupid Dago bastard," one called.
"Go back where you come from.
We don't want your kind here."

In the Still Photograph,
Paterson, New Jersey, Circa 1950

We are standing in a backyard.
Part of a porch is visible, a lattice
heavy with roses, a small tree.
Beyond the bushes in the background,
a woman with her hand on her hip
stares at us.

My father is young. He squints
into the sun. He wears a white shirt,
a flowered tie, a pair of gabardine pants
and dress shoes. His hair is thick
and crew cut. My mother wears high-heeled
black shoes with a strap across the ankle
and nylons and a black dress
printed with large flowers,
her hair, bobbed and neat.
Her arm, bent at the elbow,
looks strong and firm.
I cannot see her expression clearly,
but I think she is smiling.
Her hand is on my sister Laura's arm,
Laura stands between them.
She is thirteen, her skin clear and beautiful.

Alex and I share a small stool
in front of the three grouped
behind us, my long hair drawn back

in a straight line. I sit
behind him. He is about seven,
slim and dressed up in imitation
of my father, except Alex wears
a bow tie. His knees look sharp
and boney through his pants,
his hands clasped together
between his knees.

Even in the standard family picture,
we do not look American.

I think of my mother's preparations:
The rough feel of the washcloth
and Lifebouy soap against my face,
the stiff, starched feel of my blouse,
the streets of Paterson, old and cracked,
the houses leaning together
like crooked teeth, the yards
that grow larger as we climb the hill,
the immigrant gardens.

We walk back home
in early evening, after the grown-ups
have espresso and anisette and
we, small jelly glasses of juice.
My brother's hand in mine, I pretend
to be grown up. Dreams
cluster around my head
like a halo, while crickets
fill the summer evening
with their shining web of song.

Connections

Some days, when the world
seems to be chasing me
with an axe and I'm driving along,
on the way home from work,
or to the post office or some other
ordinary place, I find myself
pulling into my mother's driveway
almost as though the car
decided, incredibly, to drive
toward there instead of heading
for home where the clothes wait
to be washed and the dinner cooked
and my poems wait to be placed
in clean white envelopes
and sent out to editors.
Anyway there I am, without
intending to be, knocking
on my mother's door and
she is there. She welcomes me,
smiling and criticizing,
glad to see me
even though she tells me
my hair does not look right
and why don't I wear some make up
and if she doesn't tell me,
who will? She cleans off

the already clean white table
in the basement kitchen
where she does all her cooking
(the first floor kitchen
is never used, and looks
showroom new) and takes out a cup
and pours me an espresso
without even asking and looks
in the refrigerator to see if there is anything
else that I want. She asks
about each item, warms up
some pasta and fasoli or some lentils and rice,
and sits down to talk. I marvel
at how small she is when she sits down,
her hands delicate,
with tiny bones, and her body compact.
Looking at her face, I realize,
suddenly, that she could die,
that if she were not here
for me, I would have no one
to go to for sustenance,
as I come to her, looking
for the food that satisfies
all hunger, knowing that no matter what,
she is there for me, and that I need
to have her there, as though
the world were a quaking bog
and she, the only solid place
on which to stand.

My Grandmother's Hands

I never saw them.
Once she sent a picture of herself,
skinny as a hook, her backdrop
a cobbled street and a house
of stones.
In a black dress and black stockings,
she smiles over toothless gums,
old years before she should have been,
buttoned neck to shin in heavy black.
Her eyes express an emotion
it is difficult to read.

I think of my mother's mother
and her mother's mother, traced
back from us on the thin thread of memory.
In that little mountain village,
the beds where the children
were born and the old ones died
were passed from one generation
to the next, but when my mother married,
she left her family behind. The ribbon
between herself and the past
ended with her,
though she tried to pass it on.

And my own children cannot understand
a word of the old language,

the past of the village so far
removed that they cannot find
the connection between it
and themselves, will not pass it on.
They cannot possess it,
not in the way we possessed it
in the 17th Street kitchen,
where the Italian stories and the words
fell over us like confetti.

All the years of our growing
were shaped by my mother,
the old brown rocker,
the comfort of her love
and the arms that held us
secure in that tenement kitchen,
the old stories weaving connections
between ourselves and the past,
teaching us so much about love
and the gift of self
and I wonder: Did I fail
my own children? Where
is the past I gave to them
like a gift? I have tried
to love them so that always
they will imagine that love
wrapping them, like a cashmere sweater
warm and soothing on their skin.
The skein of the past
stretches back from them to me to my mother,

the old country, the old language lost,
but in this new world, saved and cherished:
the tablecloth my grandmother made,
the dresser scarves she crocheted,
and the love she taught us to weave,
a thread of woven silk
to lead us home.

The Crow

I

The voices of the old ones follow us,
warnings in whispers,
fear fed to us in bottles
along with our milk.
The first time alone,
we stand, terrified
and perfectly still,
in the kitchen
waiting for them to come home.

II

From a distance, I am awed
by the prizes you wear
like a crown.
When I meet you, your face
is the glass in which I am reflected.
In your voice, I hear a shaking so deep
I expect you to fly apart.
Though our names, changed by marriage,
are anonymous, the immigrant faces
line up in our heads. We count them,
compulsively, as if they were beads.

In our ears,
a voice,
connected to us like a cord,
whispers
you aren't really very much
you guinea, you wop,
so we struggle
to blot out the sound of the crow
who sits on our shoulder and laughs,

blot out the voice
that belittles all we do,
and drives us to be best.
My daughter she's ugly
but smart.

III

I tell you
about the reading with the poet
of the beautiful hair who keeps tossing
her head back, that glorious mane,
while I huddle in my chair
and think of having to follow her,
to get up just after she sits down.

How my insides quake
and that hair,
but I get up and turn the joke
against myself before they can.
My mother tells me I'm beautiful
but I know she means inside.

IV

You know,
I know,
we know,
who always has to be best?
We are driven women,
and we'll never escape
the voices we carry within us.

Seventeenth Street: Paterson, New Jersey

It was almost a ceremony, the welcoming of company. The aunts and uncles, the espresso pot, the espresso poured in a dark stream into the doll-sized cups set ever so delicately in their little saucers, a small sliver of lemon rind added to float near the top, then the sugar in its bowl, the spoon, midget-sized, made especially to go with those cups and saucers, and the little clink while they stirred their coffee, the men at one end of the table. Sometimes they passed out little glasses, the size of a quarter and almost one inch high, a tiny handle attached, and my father poured whisky or brandy for them, mostly the men, but sometimes the women, too. The children, sitting between the adults, were given coffee in their cups, a drop or two of coffee and lots of milk and sugar, and they listened to the stories about their parents' friends: the wayward children, the wives who were faithful or not, the men who were fools.

Listening, wide-eyed, believing, I learned more in those moments than I could in years of school about laughter and the way of opening up to others and welcoming them in, and of the magic at the heart of ordinary lives, so that ordinary things transfigured them.

Looking back, I see that ever since, I have been searching for that sweetness, the warm bread-baking aroma, the smoothness of oil cloth, its rubbery smell, the open look of my father's face, sparks flying from him in his pleasure, my mother's hand, delicate, the charm of those moments where I rested in the luminous circle of love.

APRIL 28, 1988

Paterson: Alpha and Omega

I am twelve years old.
I am slim with new breasts
and a bra, size 32, triple A
and black slacks my mother calls dungarees,
but they're nothing like the blue jeans
the popular kids wear;
they're an inexpensive version
of those jeans and in them,
despite my new figure, I feel
awkward and uncomfortable.
I know they are the wrong kind,
and in the world of the seventh grade,
there is only one right kind.

The year I'm twelve I read
every Laura Ingalls Wilder book,
Little House on the Prairie
more real to me than the world
of 19th Street:
with its tilted stoop,
the factory across the street,
the girls who wear buckskin jackets
with fringe on them
in which they look like Daniel Boone.

When I think of 19th Street, I think of Ruthie
who used to walk home from PS 18

past my house.
One day, Ruthie walked with me to the top
of the Madison Ave hill.
At Sixth Avenue, she turned
to head for the Projects
while I went on to the Riverside Branch
of the Library. She was one of the few white kids
in our class who lived in the Projects
and who was not Italian.
She had freckles on her nose,
arrived in PS #18 in seventh grade,
and was lonely.
In one long sentence,
like the kind of sentence that
Faulkner used, one of those sentences
that goes on for paragraphs, she told me
that she was going to leave
Paterson and the Projects
and was going to move in with her wealthy aunt
and have all the clothes she could ever want
and then everyone
would want to be her friend.
Even as she spoke, I knew
she was lying, fabricating
a story she wanted to believe
so desperately
that when she was finished,
she almost believed it herself.
I cringed for her, nodded, agreed.
After that day, she avoided

me as much as she could,
looked past me
as though I didn't exist
and though she must have graduated
with us, I don't remember seeing her again
until we are sophomores at Eastside High School.

I am in Alpha classes.
Most of my classes are on the third floor.
One day, as I am walking into the building,
I see her in the front lobby.
She is standing with a runty-looking boy
in jeans and a black-leather jacket.
His pimpled face leans toward Ruthie,
and Ruthie, her back to the wall, reaches up
to him and he kisses her, a long movie-star kiss.
Her skirt is tight and cheap-looking,
her blouse is a see-through nylon,
with her breasts sticking out of it
in obvious little points, but it's her face
I remember best. While he kisses her,
her eyes are open. Accidentally, I look
right into them. I see her cringe,
a flash of shame in her face, and then,
the hot surge of defiance. I know
that she is already lost, probably was lost
even on that day three years before
when we walked up the Madison Avenue hill
and she told the story of how she would escape
from the tightening ring of her life.

Eighth Grade

Eighth grade smells of chalk dust
mingled with Miss Richmond's sultry perfume.
The feel of our smooth wooden pen holders,
the silver nibs, the black ink in our inkwells,
the initials carved into our desks and
the bottled ink, the wooden floor,
scratched and scarred, the sun falling across it
in swatches and the dust swirling
like atoms through sunlight,
the green blackout shades, the maps
on pulleys that slide down over the board
Miss Richmond in her tight sweaters,
her gold jewelry, her high heels tapping,
tapping on the wooden floor.
A sense of life seethes below the surface,
all the rows of young people
yearning for their lives to begin.

One day Miss Richmond said,
"Today I'm going to tell you
who will go on to college,"
and she went down each row and said,
"you will and you won't and you will
and you won't."
I prayed and crossed my fingers for luck
and prayed. "Please, please, let her say yes."
When she came to me, she paused,

looked at me
a minute, and then, slowly, hesitating she said,
"You probably will."
Her hesitancy burns in my memory,
a wound that will never heal,
a taste in my mouth cruel and bitter as tin.

My Sister

When we were little, my sister
climbed trees, disappeared
after school with our cousin Philip
and the other boys
from our neighborhood.
Extroverted and practical, she leaped
into action, did not think too much.
She gloried in doing:
the tree climbed;
the tree house built;
the baseball game played.

When my sister turned twelve
she grew into a size 36D.
She walked languidly,
laughing
and joking with the other girls
outside the school,
but she came right home.

The boys who had been her friends watched her;
they waved casually and turned away,
but for a long time,
they did not look at one another.
The words for what they felt,
slipped through their fingers,
burning like sand at high noon.

Thinking About the Intricate Pathways
of the Brain

This snail shell is smooth and cool
in my hand, smooth as the slide
in the playground at the Riverside Oval,
the silver surface slippery
so that I slid to the ground in a rush
that took my breath away.
The inside shell is reached
through a curved lip
that forms a laughing or
sneering mouth,
and inside, a small protected curve,
and in the deepest
part of it, shadows.

I think if you could travel into it
deep enough, if you could take that journey
to the center, you'd discover
the witches waiting
with their chants and runes,
but if we gave them names,
they'd be able to escape,
like all the fears of which we are ashamed
and all the memories that lie
in the rabbit warrens
of the brain,
pathways that lead

to the witches with their
bags full of the past.

The self that is still
six years old is afraid
of heights
and of the older child
pushing the swing higher and
the laughter and terror caught
in our throats and the sky
washed in blue light moving, moving,
our legs reaching up
toward leafy trees and the perfect
puffy clouds of a July morning.

JANUARY 23, 1991

Columbus and the Road to Glory

In fourth grade, we chanted
"In Fourteen Hundred and Ninety-two,
Columbus sailed the ocean blue."
We recited the names of his ships,
the *Nina,* the *Pinta,* the *Santa Maria,*
and gave them back on test after test.
In our history books, Columbus was a hero,
part of the fabric of our American lives,
the lump in our throat when we heard
"The Star Spangled Banner" or
recited the "Pledge of Allegiance."

In Paterson, my father joined the Societa Cilentanna
formed by those Southern Italians
spewed out of mountain villages in Campagnia,
those people
that Henry Cabot Lodge called an "inferior species,"
though they were welcome in America,
cheap, unskilled labor for the jobs
no one else wanted.

My father was grateful
to get a job as a dyer's helper in a silk mill.
And when he hurt his back lifting
the heavy rolls of silk,
he became a night watchman in a school
and when he could no longer

walk the rounds ten times a night,
he got a job in a rubber factory,
gauging the pressure on steam boilers
to make sure they didn't explode.
He worked the night shift for nineteen years,
the boilers so loud he lost 90 %
of the hearing in both ears.

My father, who at eighty-six still balances
my checkbook,worked for a man
who screamed at him
as though he were a fool,
but by teaching himself the basic laws of the U. S. A.,
he learned to negotiate the system
in his broken English,
spoke up for the immigrants
when they were afraid to speak,
helped them sell property in Italy
or send for their wives and children.

On Columbus Day, dressed
in his one good suit,
his shirt, starched and white,
his dark-colored, sedate tie,
appropriate for solemn occasions,
my father stood at the podium,
loving America, believing it to be
the best and most beautiful country
in the world,
a place where his children
and the children of the others

could go to school, get good jobs.
On Columbus Day,
he could forget the laughter
of the Americans who spit at him
on the street, called him
"Dago, Guinea, Wop, Gangster,
Garlic Eater, Mafioso,"
their eyes sliding sideways
when they came near
and the rules –
"No Italians need apply."

For those Italians, living
in their tenements, surviving ten hours a day
at menial jobs, Columbus Day was their day
to shine, like my father's tuba, polished
for the occasion, my father, grinning
and marching, practicing his patriotic speech.

When I see the Italians' need to cling
to Columbus as their hero, I remember
that the biggest mass lynching
in American history was of Italians
and I remember the Italians of Frankfurt, Illinois,
dragged from their houses and beaten and lynched,
and their houses burned to the ground,
and the Italians lynched in Wiltsville, Ohio
and New Orleans and Florida
but most of all, I remember the men at the Societa,
the way they brought Columbus out once a year,
dusted him off, and presented him

to the world as their hero,
so that on that one day, they, too,
could walk tall and be proud.

And in this year of political correctness,
when I am asked to sign a petition
written by Italian American Writers
boycotting Columbus, I am angry
and I wonder: Have things changed so much for us?
Why are we always last in line, either ginzoes
in gold chains or mafiosos, found guilty
by reason of our names?
Now even this one day
set aside for Italian pride
is being ripped from our hands.

"Sta zitta, Don't make trouble!
Non far mala figura," my mother always said
but I say: Let us tell our mothers *"Sta zitta,"*
Let us tell them we don't care about *mala figura.*
Let us put the pieces of Columbus back together,
even if the cracks show, the imperfections.

Let us pick up our flawed hero,
march him through the streets of the city,
the way we carried the statue
of the Blessed Virgin at Festa.
Let us forget our mother's orders,
not to make trouble,
not to call attention to ourselves,
and in honor of my father and the men of the *Società,*

and in honor of my mother and the courage
and pride she taught me,
I say: No to being silent,
No to calling us names
No to giving up Columbus,
we have a right
with our Italian American voices
to celebrate our American lives.

The Leavetaking

To my son

I thought I could buy him happiness
all wrapped up in gold foil and ribbon.
And now, when he hurls it all in my face,
when he tells me, "Leave me alone.
I don't need you anymore,"
it takes me a week to hear.

He is taking his bureau and bed,
packing his models and books
in boxes labelled John
and putting them in the attic.
I want to cry, but I am turning
his room into my study,
and I will let him go.
I will not tell him
how to spend his money
or how to organize his new life.
I will pretend not to notice
that after this move,
he will not return to this house.
He will come back only for short visits,
sleep on the new day bed in my study,
a guest in the room that has always been his.

And I will be shy with him,
as I try to replace the picture
of the child I held and comforted

with this one, of the man
whose life is cut off from my own,
connected only in subterranean ways
with the child in the past,
clutching his matchbox toys in his small fist
and building towers with plain wooden blocks,
while the remains of the past are packed
in brown cardboard boxes labelled John.

I watch him. He waves goodbye absently,
his gray eyes fixed on the new world ahead.
I remain behind, a cardboard silhouette in a doorway,
knowing all the tears in the world
cannot alter this leavetaking, necessary and final.

AUGUST 12, 1987

Out of the Window of My Classroom

Today looking at rain through a window
and brown buildings and triangles
of clipped grass, I see that nothing,
except my name, is truly mine.
All the things I thought to hold forever
the people I have loved. First my son John
moving into his life with the speed of a comet,
the distance between us larger than the space
between Mars and Venus so that I hear his voice
coming toward me from a far place,
and Jennifer, daughter of my dearest dream,
whose voice reaches toward me across phone wires,
the cord between growing thinner
with each day: like pulled taffy, it stretches
and stretches, though I know that soon it, too, will break.
Even my mother, who has always seemed so strong,
suddenly shrinks: her eyes
get smaller with each day. Blinded
by cataracts, she peers at a world
drowning in milky light, and you,
whom I thought to hold after all others
had gone, you grow stooped
and old, years before your time.

Lament for Lost Time

Tonight I wish that I could make
the years roll back for my father,
who complains, while his hands tremble,
about not being able to tie his own shoes.
He rants against his legs so weak
and nearly useless, his swollen feet.
His eyes, hooded like a bird's, are feverish,
"stunate," like someone
who is being battered.
His face has a slash of color
across too-white skin.
In the chair next to him,
my mother lies curled,
holding a hot water bottle
wrapped in flannel, her face
white and dry as a communion wafer.
"Pray I'll be O.K.,"
she says, "or what will happen?"
She means what will happen
to your father? But when she sees
my panic, she shakes the fear
from her eyes and rises to comfort me.

Home Movies

In the old movie, 1957, we are dancing.
Our new house seems so beautiful.
The street, tree-lined and fragrant,
looks like a country lane,
and outside our bedroom window,
the Japanese cherry tree blooms.
We have just moved from
the 19ᵗʰ Street tenement
with its cement back yard,
small as a handkerchief.

I see myself lying full length
on the sofabed in the cellar.
I read in *Seventeen* magazine
about a young woman who lived
in a "modest" bungalow.
In the picture I see it is exactly like our house,
with its screened-in front porch,
its boxy living room and dining room.
its two bedrooms with room enough in them
for a double bed
and a small dresser.

How our eyes change as we grow older.
The world around us blurs,
but the world that lives in our minds
grows sharper, the picture clear

and focused. We notice details
we had missed before.

Looking back, I see my mother.
She is young, shapely, sensuous.
She dances with my brother.
She is laughing.
My sister twirls around me.
My brother chases us, saying,
"Look! There's Cletus! Let's get him,"
picking an imaginary flea out of air.

Watching the film unwind,
I feel time rushing past
like a waterfall.
The people in the movie
seem so far from us,
their clothes awkward,
out of style,
their faces untouched.

Generations

Every day I'd read to John from those small books
I'd get at the supermarket
or the cloth books I'd buy at toy stores,
and I remember Dennis reading the *Wizard of Oz*
books to him, but even when he still fit in the wicker
clothes basket, he'd rest in there and read a book,
his large, solemn gray eyes
absorbed in the print,
the page turning rapidly under his hand,
and he, able to tell the story
of what he'd read, almost word for word.
He liked to have us read to him,
charmed by the rhythm of the spoken word,
though even at four he could have read it faster himself,
and I think of him today,
singing chorus after chorus of "Old MacDonald Had
a Farm" because his daughter stops crying
when she hears his voice singing that song,
her large solemn eyes fixed on him,
her face, with that attentive, listening look,
her intelligence evident even at six months.
I think of my son, his daughter, the years ahead,
Caroline snuggled into the crook of his arm
and him reading to her, patiently,
though he is impatient with all else
and easily bored,

and she, loving the sound of his voice,
his arm curving around her,
his hands on her fiery hair.

Song for Caroline

Caroline, Caroline Paige,
grand-daughter,
I treasure your curious stare,
your sturdy pushing legs.
I watch your mother's face
when she holds you,
lit from within as I was
when I held your father,
that Johnson's baby powder scent,
the warm smooth feel of your skin
against my mouth,
and for one moment,
sliding back in time,
I am young again
and you are my child.

In 1965 in that Rutgers apartment,
I sat through the long, hacking night,
holding your father
and rocking into dawn light.
How warm he was in my arms,
how sure I was I would keep him forever.
Now I hold you,
the child I held so long ago
vanished:
Little flower,
little chirping bird,

you watch the world
through big, solemn eyes
drinking everything in,
storing it up
the seriousness of it all,
and you, your sudden smile
when you look at your father
as though all the glory
in the universe
were gathered in his hands.

Caroline, Caroline Paige,
Granddaughter,
today when I hold you,
you burrow into the curve
of my neck, and I wonder
when you are older
will you come to me
with your secrets
and your sorrows?
Will we become friends
a little while
before you rush into your life?
Already you are trying to walk,
your legs, too delicate to hold
your slender body,
want to walk anyway,
your feet moving though air,
practicing the motion
that will take you away.

We gather in a circle around you,
as if you were a fire and we, needing
your warmth against the chill.
Blue as pansies, as violets, your eyes
fix on each of us in turn,
your father, mother, grandfather and me.
We are awed by you, your copper hair,
your impish mouth, your legs,
so strong and wirey, and you,
and all of us, so pleased with you.
We smile at you,
this blessing, this magic charm,
this energy which crackles
in the room, so new, so new.

Paradise Motel

I wait in the Paradise Motel in this small Vermont town brimming with gray early morning light. I am waiting for the woman who has been assigned by this college to pick me up, though I'd rather eat breakfast alone. I realize I'm hungry and begin to get annoyed that she can't get herself here on time. When she arrives, we are awkward with each other. Her pants are black and white checked. They are badly wrinkled and her blouse appears tossed on. She wears a black sweater that covers her rear end. Her hair is frazzled into ringlets; it looks burned, and hangs in curled strings around her face and down her back. I try to carry on a conversation, try to find some common ground on which we can rest.

After we sit down in the Cozy Kettle Cafe and order breakfast, my attempts at conversation begin to break the uncomfortable stiffness between us. She mentions some of my poems, says how much they remind her of her mother. Then she spills out words about her life, her boyfriend whom she met on the street. She and her friend were walking down main street, she says, and she saw him pass and he said, "Hello: How are you doing tonight?" She answered and they started talking and they went to the park and sat there till 3 A.M. She's been dating him ever since. He works in a factory that makes coat hangers. He lived with a woman and has an eight-year-old son. They weren't getting along, she says, and he wanted to break up with her, but she trapped him by getting pregnant. He left her when she was eight months pregnant. "I love him," this girl says. "He makes me feel good about myself. He's the only one. We are going to get married." I say, "You are very young, try to be very sure," knowing that she will not hear. Thinking: a blue collar worker in a country where manufacturing is dying. Thinking: poor girl, poor girl. Thinking: he left his girl when she was eight months pregnant. "See," she says, "I have this hair on my chin, a lot of hair and a moustache. I've always been conscious of it, thought people would mind, but he doesn't. See, he doesn't. He shaves the hair on my chin for me." Her eyes have darkened and softened. They are now blue/green and her face, with that soft light, almost beautiful.

I am moved by seeing how much she needs to be loved, enough to blind herself to his flaws – the warning signals: his mother who lives in a filthy trailer and has piles of old junk in the yard; the deserted girlfriend, the custody battle, the dead end job. "I know I'm too fat," she says, " but I hate exercise. My mother says I have childbearing hips." "I am the decision maker," she says, "I cook and clean for him now. It's like having a baby. He needs me to take care of him."

I tell her about myself when I was her age. How shy and awkward I was, how I saw myself as ugly and fat. "You'll be suprised," I say, "how much more beautiful you'll appear when you look back at pictures in fifteen years. You won't believe it."

The long baggy sweater she wears is designed to cover her body, which, when she stands, I see is full-breasted and curvacious. In different clothes, with her hair clean and straight and falling free, her face without the closed, clod-like expression, her face, open and soft, her eyes shining, as they are now, she would be striking and beautiful. I can feel that even she knows she's marrying to keep from facing her life, running into marriage as a refuge where she can say she is married, loved, where she can feel beautiful. I hope that she cannot see my fear for her, or the pity that floods over me. She leaves me at the hotel where I will wait for the artsy student who will pick me up to take me to the train. "I'm glad you talked to me," she says. "I feel better about myself. I hope you'll come back soon." Her eyes look bruised, dark-circled, and in the parking lot, surrounded by imposing mountains and drowning in gray light, I hug her. "Good luck," I say. Her eyes fill with tears. "Yes," she says. "Yes."

Requiem for a Four-Year-Old

Mark Warner was four years old
when he died in a Paterson slum. These days
even the people in his old neighborhood
can't remember his name.
"All I know is a little boy died here.
Nobody don't talk about it."
The words are spoken casually by a tall, slender woman
with orange-red nail polish. She gives her name
only as "Tee." No last name. On this block
of Broadway in Paterson, where used crack vials
are scattered at the curb and winos
hang out all day outside a liquor store,
people don't give their full names,
Tee is nineteen. She lives in apartment 6,
the same apartment where Mark Warner lived and died.
Standing on the rickety front stoop under a broken win-
dow, Tee says: "Everybody here now wasn't here then."

"Sometimes I just give him a couple of slaps,"
Michael Thomas, Mark's stepfather says.
"But this time I hit him a while."
In the color pictures of Mark Warner,
Mark's lower lip is split
and large purple bruises distort most of his face
and body.
Four round scars,
old cigarette burns, mark his buttocks.

The coroner believes the welts on his back
are from a whipping with a belt or a wire loop.
Assistant Passaic County Prosecutor,
Marilyn Zdobinski, shakes her head in disgust.
"These are the crimes
that people do not think happen,"
Zdobinski says.
"But people beat kids every day."

Last week, Mark's twenty-one-year-old mother,
Alvira Warner Thomas, stood silently
in an empty Passaic County Courtroom;
She was sentenced to four years probation
and ordered to seek counseling.
Michael Thomas was sentenced to ten years
without parole. "He is very depressed,"
his lawyer says.

From an article in *The Herald & News*
Paterson, N. J., FEBRUARY 13, 1988

In Falling Light, Paterson

In falling light, Paterson sky
is an incredible blue so bright
and deep it seems painted on even as it slides
toward pale pink against the ochre brick
mills. I drive past the rococo arches
of the Church painted in lavender and gray,
drive down to Oliver and then, into Mill,
past Federici's green and decaying Dublin Spring sculpture
and onto Route 80 where the stars
thicken into clusters in the blazing sky
and the lights of the city float in a sea
of space. The weight
of the day lifts, light as a gauze
shawl, off my shoulders, all
heaviness falling away before the
dizzying panorama, luminous
and vast.

MARCH 27, 1988

Ma, Who Told Me You Forgot
How to Cry

Soothsayer,
healer,
tale-teller,
there was nothing you could not do.

In your basement kitchen,
with the cracked brown and yellow tiles,
the sink on metal legs,
the big iron stove with its pots simmering,
the old Kelvinator from 1950,
the metal kitchen table and plastic chairs,
I'd watch you roll out dough for *pastichelle*.
"Be quiet," you'd say,
and work at super speed.

Today, when we walk into your hospital room,
you do not speak of your illness,
do not mention the doctor
who tells you bluntly,
"You have three months, at most, to live."

Your shrewd, sharp eyes watch us,
but you do not cry .

Soothsayer,
healer,
tale-teller,
always ready with a laugh and a story,
ready to offer coffee, cakes,
advice at your oval kitchen table,
your chair pulled close and your hands
always full.

We are like little children gathered
around your bed. Al, with his doctor's bag
full of tricks and medicine,
Laura, in her nurse's uniform,
her hands twisting, and me,
my head full of words
that here, in this antiseptic room,
are no use, no use at all.

We wait for you
to get up out of that bed,
to start bossing us around,
the way you always did.
Tell us a story
with a happy ending,
one in which the oil
of *Santo Rocco* that you put on
your swollen belly each night
works its elusive miracle.

Soothsayer,
healer,
tale-teller,
there was nothing you could not do.
Tell us again how the bluebirds
came to sing at your window
that January, when Al was so sick
all the doctors said he'd die.

But I Always Got Away

My mother dreams that two people,
one a bald-headed man, have grabbed her.
They try to push her into a small windowless room.
They will never let her out.

"No! No!" she screams at them,
lifts up two baseball bats
which miraculously appear in her hands,
and beats them on the head, very hard,
"but not enough to kill them," them she assures us,
"just enough to knock them out."

"I escape," she says, "and leave them
behind me on the floor, their mouths
open." She demonstrates, opening her mouth
wide, the white line around her lips clear,
her face pale as white flour.

"You have three months, at most, to live,"
the doctor tells her, but it is one month already,
and she is beginning to get up, beginning to hope.
"I got away," she laughs and for a moment,
we are drawn into her belief. "I had the same dream
three times, but I always got away."

Ma, I Think of You Waiting

Each day for the health aide
who arrives at your house at 7 A.M. and leaves
again at 10 A.M. In the afternoon,
sometimes Orlando visits
and then at 6, Al arrives.
By 6:30 P.M., you begin to wait
for me. By the time I arrive
at 8, you are leaning forward
in your chair; you are restless.
"Are you in pain?" I ask.
"No, just uncomfortable," you say.
You want to go to bed, gear up
to get out of your chair,
and are breathing hard after walking
five feet to your bed.
I help you undress, lift your clothes
over your head. You close your eyes,
your face pale and strained.
"I'm too much trouble for you kids,"
you say. I protest, stroking
your hand that each day loses
more flesh. You move over
onto your side, then onto your
back, move your legs, and then, back
onto your side again. "I'm just
not comfortable," you say. "nervous.

I don't know why."
Al says, "I hope she'll live till the new year"
but I tell Laura, "I don't know.
She seems so weak."

After I have given you your pills,
warmed your milk, given Dad
his cocoa and helped him
into bed, I get ready to leave you.
The last thing I see before I walk
out the door is your face in profile,
your nose sharper than I remembered
the bones of your skull prominent
your lips moving in prayer.

Visiting My Mother

Last night, I visited my mother and all the lies I've been telling myself about how this medicine will work and how she's going to get better are lies, and part of me knows it and the other part does not want to believe it. Watching her I see her arm is thin and that she takes two sips of lemonade after saying how thirsty she is, and then says she doesn't want any more.

Laura has just given her Demerol and as it takes effect, she perks up. She has dark brown smudges under her eyes and her face is hollowed out. She has taken out her teeth, though she has always boasted that she never takes them out, and she tells us stories non-stop, the past filled with details she has never told us before.

When I was born, she tell us, my father walked down to the grocery store on Fourth Avenue to call the doctor. Meanwhile, she looked down and there I was, my head and shoulders emerging. "What a surprise," she says. For a moment, she is so lucid, her eyes shining, that we forget how weak she was just a few minutes ago.

When Alessandro was born, she was in the hospital in a basement delivery room and all the women were being taken in to give birth but no one came to get her. She screamed until she got the attention of a young intern who delivered the baby. The doctor never arrived. Alex had a head full of black hair when he was born. She smiles and says, "I took that young doctor's hand and said, 'Thank you. You are so good.' I wonder what happened to him? Maybe he's dead. Well, God bless him, if he's not dead."

"You know," she muses, "when you were little babies, they had a nurse who took care of you. I brought you to the school and she was there and she weighed you and measured you and gave you your shots. She had this little book that she wrote in the weight and height and which shots and then, she'd put in a gold star if the baby was well and had grown. I kept that book. Used to take it out and look at it. So nice. All those gold stars. I had it a little while ago. It was nice," she says and laughs.

Grief

It's more than three months since my mother died, and I realize how grief comes to us over and over, how it catches us unawares, how it is the small things that make us remember, the dented pot in my mother's pantry, the sad, threadbare towels, the unused nightgowns folded neatly in her bureau.

Sometimes, on the way to work, coming down River Street arching under the railroad bridge just past Our Lady of Lourdes, I remember my mother. I am driving and crying, wanting her here with me now, and I think of the times I did not call her, the times I was annoyed that she called me every day, and would give anything now to have her call me, to have her be there when I climb the stairs to her kitchen, to find there, not Irena, the Polish lady who stays with my father because he cannot be left alone, but my mother, busy and strong as she once was, energy radiating off her, her spirit courageous and indomitable so I think she can't be dead, she can't be dead, not when I still need her, and I think of how she told me she was going to have cataract surgery. We are sitting at her kitchen table the week before her operation, and we are talking about some other things, and suddenly, I say, "So when are you leaving, Ma?" "Leaving?" she says, and laughs, we both laugh, but we are both afraid, superstitious that this slip of my tongue, this question I didn't know I was going to ask, means she is going to die, but I shrug off this dire premonition, slap away the insistent voice in my head, though I should know better by now, know that I ignore the voice at my peril, and that my mother and I share this instinctive knowledge of the future that floats around us thin as veils, invisible to all eyes but ours. When she was dying, when she died and came back, she told us about the garden where her mother and sisters walked, the beautiful garden, peaceful and calm, where she sees her mother and sisters, bathed in light that transforms them to creatures magnificent in their beauty, and she says they were there and walked together, and then she turns to me, and says, "you were there, too." I think that maybe in this, too, she was right, that maybe I am going to die soon, but I tell myself no, no, I can't die yet, I have so much more I want to do, and I think of holding my niece Debbie's baby, his head resting on my chest, and her father saying how much Mom would have loved seeing him, this bruiser of a boy, this child with Debbie's mouth and the shoulders of a football player and his huge beautiful eyes who so reminds me of Debbie as a baby. How my mother would have smiled at him, laughed with us when he snored, been happy to see us all there together in Laura's kitchen, our eyes filling with grief over our loss of her.

Heritage

I'm like those Russian peasant dolls
made of lacquered wood where the larger dolls open
to reveal smaller dolls, until finally
the smallest doll of all stands, unseamed and solid.

When you open me up: my mother, her mother,
my daughter, my son's daughter. It could go on for ever,
the way I carry them inside me.
Only their voices emerge, and when
I speak to my daughter,
I hear their words tangled in my own.

Ma, when you died, I thought I'd lost you forever;
grief washes over me
when I pass your barren garden and remember
the tomatoes that grew so wildly while you
watched from the bedroom where you were dying;
or when I walk into your basement kitchen
and see that it is grimy with neglect;
or when I see Dad sitting in the big recliner,
his legs covered by a blanket you crocheted
and a picture of you propped up
on the table next to him,
but when I open myself
you are still there inside me and I am safe,
even though I cannot drive to your house
or sit down while you pour me an espresso.

This is the way it is with me –
you are nested inside me,
your voice a whisper that grows clearer
with each day.

On Reading Susan Toth's Blooming

Wind pointers twirl through past
summers in the Seventeenth Street garden,
turned earth, blacker than coal in the cellar,
smell of earth, tart and cool as
the lemonade we made
in a big glass pitcher,
lemon halves whirling
like snow in a paperweight.

Once I held one of those crystal weights in my hand.
How I loved the snow
falling softly over the perfect village and people,
the white New England Church, the small,
winding road and all of it, protected
by a glass, the way the past is for me,
boundaried and safe,
a place where I am held by hands
that love me and that I trust
never to let go.

Where I Come From

This twig, bent into a miniature bow, is cracked and peeling in spots, its bark almost silver with black dots, and in the peeled spots, the wood tan and white. Rough to the touch, it is nobby with black knots shaped like flowers or lips, but the ends are jaggedly torn, as though a careless hand snapped the twig from the tree.

I think of my mother, the doctor who says she is dying, but she hangs on to life, her body growing smaller with each day, her eyes, round and black. We sit together on the edge of her bed; her legs don't touch the floor. We look at pictures that she saved in a plastic folder; her sister, Giuseppina, who died in childbirth more than sixty years ago; her mother, spare and slim as a needle and dressed all in black, her hair pulled back in a knot at the nape of her neck, her sister, Lena, at fifty, squat and shapeless from childbearing, her face round, her skin clear and smooth, though she looks seventy in her loose black dress and black old lady shoes.

"So many stories I could tell," my mother says, "so many," and she tells us stories we had not heard before, as though her life, in all its nobbiness, bent like this twig, arched and beautiful, is being torn away. She peels at the crusty bark that has made her always the sturdy one, the one we all came to for help, and now, the wood beneath revealed, tan and clean. Her hand reaches out toward me, and when I take it and hold it in mine, it feels so light, her bones so delicate, I am surprised when it does not disappear.

Afterword

Maria Mazziotti Gillan poetic universe is spun out of the world of everyday life. Its strength is in the familiar, its marvels are revealed by where that familiar leads us. Where we go with her.

She makes her domain out of the domestic, and then holds that *domus* as a mirror to show us her humanity, and ours. The poems are a woman's poems: mother and daughter both figure large in them in a way that is blessedly unique to our time, and our telling (tale-ing). The strength of the work is in its simplicity and directness.

Where Maria Mazziotti Gillan "comes from" is clearly imaged here: the fig tree, the basement kitchen, the ghetto streets of Paterson, the special espresso service with its tiny silver spoons, her father's demeaning jobs, the sacred tenacity of her people – theirs ways of being and of being together. Where she is now going, as a poet and a woman, is barely hinted at, but it comes through strong: because it is the journey we are all – uprooted as we are on a vast and windy continent – now making.

It is at once a journey home to ourselves, our ancestral customs and beliefs, and outward, to whatever possibilities await us in this ravaged global village, where the music and the laughter are as ceaseless as the cries of pain. It is a journey backwards and forwards at once, like all poetic journeys, and Maria Mazziotti Gillan's work illuminates a part of the road for us.

DIANE DI PRIMA
December 15, 1994
San Francisco

Acknowledgments

Some of the poems in this volume appeared previously in *Flowers from the Tree of Night* (Chantry Press, Midland Park, NJ, 1980, 1981); *Winter Light* (Chantry Press, 1985, 1987); *The Weather of Old Seasons* (Cross-Cultural Communications, Merrick, NY, 1988, 1993); *The Dream Book: Writings by Italian-American Women* (edited by Helen Baroloni: Schochen, NY, 1985); *From the Margin: Writings in Italian Americana* (edited by Paul Giordano, Antony Tamburri and Fred Gardaphé, Purdue University Press, 1990); *Il viaggio delle donne* (edited by Giovanna Capone and Denise Nico Leto, *Sinister Wisdom,* 1990); *The Voices We Carry* (edited by Mary Jo Bona, Guernica Editions, Montreal-Toronto, 1994); *On Prejudice* (edited by Daniella Gioseffi, Doubleday, NY, 1993); *La Bella Figura: Choices* (Malafemmina Press, San Francisco, 1993); *Speaking for Peace* (edited by Ruth Jacobs, 1993); *Cries of the Spirit* (Boston, Beacon Press, 1991); and the following journals: *Poetry Australia, Lips, North Dakota Quarterly, Negative Capability, Voices in Italian Americana, La Bella Figura, Slow Dancing, The Croton Review, The Journal of Women and Spirituality, Studia Mystica, The Passaic Review, The Chester Jones Foundation Awards Anthology, Almanacco, Trapani Nuovo, La Terza Pagina, The New Moon Review, Free Inquiry, Earth's Daughters, Ora Madre, Sri Chinmoy Awards Anthology.*

«L'IMPRIMEUR»

• Cap-Saint-Ignace
• Sainte-Marie (Beauce)
  Quebec, Canada
  1995